In the Willing Dirt

poems by

Jade Bradbury

Purple Passion Press • Los Gatos • California

In the Willing Dirt
Copyright © 2019 by Jade Bradbury

Editor: Erica Goss
Cover Art: Bill Kalogeros
Cover Design: Bill Kalogeros

Founder/Production Manager/Page Design:
Victoria M. Johnson

All rights reserved.
No part of this book may be reproduced or transmitted in any form or by any means, electronic or mechanical, including photocopying, recording or any other information storage and retrieval system, without written consent from Purple Passion Press.

Inquiries and correspondence should be emailed to:
info@PurplePassionPress.com

ISBN:
978-1-7331260-0-7

Purple Passion Press
http://PurplePassionPress.com
http://www.facebook.com/PurplePassionPress
http://twitter.com/Purple_P_Press

For Bill and Sheleigh.

And with gratitude for *ohana,* the family of friends whose love keeps me both grounded and aloft.

Acknowledgements

Grateful acknowledgement to the editors of the following journals, in which these poems first appeared.

Name 'splain: Canto I
Published in "*spring mother tongue, Poetic Voices of Santa Clara County,*" edited by Arlene Biala, County Poet Laureate, 2017.

Postwar Blues, 1944: Canto II
Published in "*spring mother tongue, Poetic Voices of Santa Clara County,*" edited by Arlene Biala, County Poet Laureate, 2017.

Letter to God (After Hafiz)
Published by The Literary Nest 2015

Special thanks for support and encouragement, in alphabetical order to: Sally Ashton; Anam Cara Friends; Arlene Biala; Laurie Barna; Bay Area Book Artists; Poetess Kalamu Chaché; Champagne Literary Society; Kosrof and Kit Chantikian; Bill Cozzini, Lucille Lang Day; David Denny; Dave Eisbach; Marilyn Fahey; Flash Fiction Forum; Kay Flavell; Pat Fox; Jerry Garner; Kris Goodrich; Erica Goss; Parthenia Hicks; Amado Hipol; Leslie Hoffman; Victoria M. Johnson; Bill Kalogeros; Pratibha Kelapure; Lita Kurth; Anne Lamborn; Light-Worker Poets; Pushpa MacFarlane; Nancy Martin; Tania Martin; Lesa Medley; Amy Meier; Margaret More; Ann Muto; New Pacific Studio; Flo Oy; Carol Park; Betty Peck; Peerless Poets; Robert Pesich; Sheleigh K. Peters; Poetry Center San Jose; Poetry Lounge; Purple Passion Press; Mary Ruth Quinn; Anna, Sarah and Merina Rainville; Laynee Reyna; Lynnette Vega; Sam and Shereel Washington; Well-RED Reading Series; Barbara Wesson; Amanda Williamson; Willow Glen Poetry Project; and Writers Feedback Group.

Table of Contents

Editor's Note	vi
Part One	
The Grammar of Dirt & Probability	9
Lullaby for My Two-Year Old Self	10
Name 'splain: Canto I	11
My Mother's Buddha	12
Journey (For Sheleigh)	14
Two if by Sea	15
All Flesh is Grass	16
Burning Love	18
Did You Feel It?	19
In Time of Drought (For Bill)	20
Sky Rivers	21
Love Among the Ruins	22
Postwar Blues, 1944: Canto II	24
Part Two	
Ocean Park Dreamscapes	27
Letter to God (After Hafiz)	30
If Emily Had Been So Stricken	31
Malady as Metaphor	32
Autograph Tree Rescue	33
How We Know	35
Stones of Tohono O'odham	36
Star Maps I	38
Das Boot: Sixth Extinction Log	39
Crows Before the Fall	40
Request	41
About the Author	43

Editor's Note

It gives me great pleasure to introduce this book. Jade Bradbury, friend and fellow poet, has written a work of grace and insight. I witnessed some of these poems come to life, from idea to draft to finished work, and I'm happy to see them assembled in this richly satisfying collection.

Filled with humor and spirit, the poems in this book illuminate the toil and tenderness of a well-lived life. Appreciation for Nature, as well as a good dose of respect for its subtle and powerful systems, weaves a thread throughout the book. "Journey," for example, describes the process of lichen attaching itself to a stone ("the rock does not resist") and ends as the stone, eroded into "a micro-landscape," washes into the sea. "All Flesh is Grass" echoes this sentiment of decay, of wearing down, of the body reassembling itself for "what prevails despite impermanence."

The natural world, with its delights, dangers, and enigmas, plays a prominent role in this book. In "How We Know," the speaker tries to grasp her enigmatic encounters with animals: "a fox, two hawks, a bear, / and five boars." In "Burning Love," Bradbury tackles the question, "What would you take from a burning house?" As a fire threatens her home, the speaker discovers that she has grabbed "three quick-found keepsakes:" "my wedding / bracelet, a one-eyed, love-worn teddy bear, / and favorite bedside book of poems to read." The reader wonders what things, precious and seemingly random, she would have assembled in that particular state of mind.

Jade Bradbury's poems do not shy away from difficult questions, probing the mysterious underpinnings that connect us all, no matter how disquieting. These are poems to savor and return to again and again.

— Erica Goss, May 2019

Part One

The Grammar of Dirt & Probability

Begin in earnest, plant something
                    in the willing dirt,
cultivate a crop through stewardship,
                    as in not to own
either dirt or crop, their issue yours
                    to tend, not keep.
And what if you knew how it'd begin
                    and end, yet still
agreed to see it all the way through until
                    its expected course
became yours to test, that the outcome
                    of your intent can
alter & set what will be, what will have been
                    a grammatical flaw
that defies a law of physics you don't
                    properly divine as yet—
changed in the fullness of time and now expressed
                    as dormant energy:
You who plant poems to feed a weary world
                    at war with itself;
you who've been living as if this plot of dirt
                    is subject to your will.

Lullaby for My Two-Year Old Self

You are already inside her head,
little one, thinking, thinking,
worried and lonely while
she sleeps, you wander
slowly through ill-lit rooms, wanting
the solace of her company.
You feel the soundless intervals,
holes in shadowed pre-war
halls where Mama agreed we'd stay
when Daddy's gone, is gone away.
But sometimes she sings sweetly,
and you sing too, for years
and years to come until your throat
worn raw-bone thin, cries out
for relief, for time, for more time…
but softly she dies, and so will you,
so will you.

Name 'splain: Canto I

My name is Jade, like the stone,
I learned to say, not Jane
for goodness sake. The lame cover
of a postwar, non-Asian child,
born of a storm in the deep, deep
South, not yet apprised a jade
is also an emaciated horse,
a woman of "ill-repute", according
to dictionaries of course. But when
I learned those other turns, I
kept it to myself, burden of proof
on me to show the heart of stone —
how it glows, hardened and honed,
jade of ancient lore, precious
gem, earth star of rescued light
from holes of blackness, astride
the winding Milky Way. Jade
like the stone, I like to say,
this is how I roll.

My Mother's Buddha

My mother's seated Buddha traveled
by truck, Seattle to Los Gatos
with us, a sweet smile upon his
youthful face, as if eternal
grace becomes him, even though
his gilded outer shell hides
woody impermanence within.
We're complicit with his
mudra: fingers of one hand
touching the earth, upturned palm
at his lap, he's poised between
the heavens above and the unruly
mud below.

Driving south I relived my mother's
passing, how cancer commanded
her body's closing betrayal:
enemies inflamed all sites within,
burned her palms-up request,
ignored her plea to remain here
on earth. Her Buddha still smiling,
we'd gathered him up, set him in
the truck's above-cab window
to oversee our restive trip
through a darkly lonesome sphere.

Coming through Trinity Forest fires
by night, eyes of animals crossing
the road alight with fear and flame,
we choked on smoke and backtracked
to park in a fire-free zone, slept
fitfully near a dark meadow
rattling with snaps of grounded twigs,

scrabblings of small creatures, and
clash of dried weeds sired by searing sun,
sounding like oncoming blaze...

Now he sits in our bedroom, my
mother's Buddha, reminder of
her brave attempt to prevail while
hosting a hoard of alien cells--
in his case, tiny bugs--that can
change the course of our days;
that no amount of fervent hope
or appeal can alter when friendly
fires turn anxious with the wind,
touch the soft brown earth, fueled
and ablaze, igniting renewal.

Journey (For Sheleigh)

When lichens start
overtaking stone,
the rock does not resist,
in fact submits, or doesn't
care, preoccupied
with simply being there.
But lichen-time wears away
relentlessly and when
at last this blooming leveler
has done its reductive
deed, all is fluidity,
a micro-landscape that travels
light all down the rivers
and into the sea, its mother —
she then rimmed with tiny
stars upon her moonlit
beaches.

Note: Lichens are known to have been among the first plants to emerge from the seas to make their home on the land. The ontogeny that created mountains — also once beneath the oceans — is ironically reversed by the steady release of acids from lichens breaking down mammoth boulders into the pearly sand often found at the seas' sparkling shores.

Two if by Sea

Here on this beach, this often
dreamed of place, listlessly shifting
as if waiting, the dreamed and
dreamer crest a pearly dune:
sensation of sailing, delicate
sand-fans pluming as each step
quick-fills with grainy intent

Sullen swathes of salt air stir
a thick silver overcast,
prelude to sea-change, a
constant at this dark-water
confluence, where ribbons
of braiding streams briskly funnel
towards consummate baptism

Ahead the low tide arches
wide and gray, glistening briefly
when water recedes. Ragged
shawls of swirling fog hover
the pummeled shelf of sand,
and I lay me down yet again
upon its long white bed

All Flesh is Grass

My therapist friend suggests
I'm the product of my gut:
ardent archivist, modern
hunter-gatherer, saver of seeds
and proofs of life, I who
compulsively collect, record,
sample, preserving the stuff
of streams, of mountains,
of objects-- to extend and sustain
the slender prospect
of living on Earth forever.

But isn't this a calling, I ask,
an expression of love? Look
at me, she says, and listen closely.
Two words: *dysfunctional loyalty.*
I'm dumbstruck, saddened
by what is undeniable — my error.
In the midst of every-day
detritus and its drive toward
crushing decay, my activity
feels urgent, charged with purpose,
as if some graceless redemption
depends upon it.

Meanwhile, anxious spawns
of blooming molds and shimmering
dews bring down mountains,
walls, and the heart's arterial pathways,
tugging them back to their starts,
and what prevails despite impermanence,
is rescued by a man-made image —

an artifact—whose presence offers, if not
respite, evidence that suffering shows
a way along the curve of eternity.

And I say I know this means I'm not or
ever was but briefly unique, yet
bound to live and die in this space, sheltered
by what remains, salvaged
by what abides: *All flesh is grass.*

Burning Love

Exalting in a free fall morning, still
in nightie and coffee in hand,
I briefly catch the acrid-sere
fragrance of wood-smoke added
to a sparkling blue day, probably
ignited by remembrance of autumns
past, I thought, the blaze of false
pistachios and tall vine maples
crisply lining the cul-de-sac...but then
I see orange flower of flame blossom,
parting the roof shakes next door;
hear the vague crackling like paper
coming un-crumpled, coming alive,
our duplex divide now filling with smoke,
and my mouth too dry to say fire,
FIRE, as in those dreams, the raking
silence of closed-throat fear,
the choking smoke, harsh scent of burning
wood and wire and insulation — is anyone
inside? — 9-1-1 — where is the phone? Outside
some passing workers shut off gas,
enter with extinguisher and pull out
my shuddering neighbor, her small child...
I notice I have taken, just in case,
three quick-found keepsakes from my
adjoining, neighboring place and thrown
them in a bag like a burglar: my wedding
bracelet, a one-eyed, love-worn teddy bear,
and favorite bedside book of poems to read,
a discreet guide for starting over again.

Did You Feel It?

Once you've weathered
an earthquake, or random
act of human violence,
any rolling sensation
or unexpected motion
is thereafter subject
to re-evaluation, and you get
that earth is no longer
a sanctuary from treachery or
other unholy surprises.

Once a series of personal
reversals or a swarm
of post-traumatic tremors
rattles your peace of mind
you panic when
the Jell-O quiver beneath
your feet engages
your fight or flight instincts
as surely as when early
kith and kin faced terrors
destined to extinct them.

Once land, air, water or
mutual agreements shift
for reasons you can't know
it only seems right to respond
to embedded faults
not asking or guessing
if by flawed integrity
but why you must endure
these vexing tests
in order to live.

In Time of Drought (For Bill)

On windless days we could hear
the crying of trees, or
maybe their dying.
There was no relief. How we
ached to hear honking geese
overhead, refreshed from nearby
perc ponds. Songbirds on the wing
no longer breached the fetid air,
the cloudless sky. Only crows and
stellar jays joined our urban
sorrows, pointedly pecking at grooves
between sere pavements in vain.
And how we grieved the car-wash
duck family you shepherded once
across high traffic lanes, your arm
aloft like a crossing guard, they
(later brutally run over one night after
hours by a drive-through madman),
they who no more navigate our driven
ways. Threat of fire and dire attrition
in that hollow time stalked the avenues,
and yes, we were very afraid…
but you, yes you, were our saving grace.

Sky Rivers

The sound of rain long
withheld began to pound
into gutters bloated with debris
of the extended drought,
washing over our yearning,
our bleakest doubts, conjured
weather analysts who spoke
of atmospheric rivers,
and we imagined what's above
our planet a roiling chaotic
place, churning up towering
peaks hewn by rivers and veins
of off-shoot streams, fueling
oceanic skyscapes, pressing
down in branching fractals
to sea and land, a cosmic
embrace with molten magma
tossing and turning beneath,
where we clay, we mud-bound
surround the rightness of rain,
born by rivers in the sky.

Love Among the Ruins

When lilacs last bloomed on my
   backyard fence, I cut their
honeyed amethyst blooms to save
   them from the landlord's
eviction. The urgent fragrance
   they breathed as she yanked
their vines from the late spring
   earth still lingers in memory.

Later that heated summer my love
   and I perched back-to-
sticky-back on the little bench
   near where lilacs were felled—
we like mewling, moaning creatures
   murmuring sweetly, moist
spinal skins met ever so softly.

Then into the garden of our
   delight came a shrieking
disruption, the grim-reaping
   landlord bearing two hats,
demands we wear them against
   sunstroke, and we like tender
lilacs gave off a primal scent, fleshy,
   alert to the heartless hand
that sought to break our trance.

I wonder, Why me? Why
   everything—the pain, the love,
the certain knowledge we'll
   all be cut down eventually?

But it's because we're here,
   warming the little bench, lighting
up the yard in back, blooming
   madly in love while still
for now we may.

Postwar Blues, 1944: Canto II

My mother's first-born child departed
her warm inland sea, swimming
downstream gamely, right on down
into Laurel, Mississippi. From unlit
pulsing corridor into swampy breathless
birthing bed--darkened by lightning
strike, crash of thunder storming
through everyone's head—I came into
this world, "born alive" as my birth
certificate said, on a wild and bracing
night. Gathered there, nurses and us,
waiting for baptism by light: my first
breath and the power restored. She held
me to her breast, touching her heart,
knowing already what the naming
of her daughter will be, what they all
will say when she speaks it aloud:
Jade. "Lordy, what sort of name is that?"
Softly first, and then again, she calls
my name: Jade, precious, native
child, Jade not of the fabled orient
but born of Mississippi mud. You see,
my mother was a reader, peculiar
to say in her time and place, and Pearl
Buck's Good Earth lit her Southern
fire--mine too, as it turned out. We
each in our inward driven grace pined
for days with a difference, far-flung
dwellings we'd enter, not as strangers
but seekers, naturalized residents
of aboriginal land and rivers of change.

And so I grew into, became my name:
resistance to abrasion on Moh's
hardness scale of number 7 to 8,
yielding luminosity, a sheen of tiny
light, seeded in darkness that primed
a creative force of love that is life;
decades of writing by day, reading into
the night; forestalling final dousing
of breath, when fiery transformation
of stone to star burnishes my
tempered soul for another name. Once
the Jade of bayou mire, I'll up-sing
blues in praise of starry zones, burning
with dreams of Earth again, my
once and beloved ancestral home.

Part Two

Ocean Park Dreamscapes

Back in the early seventies we drove to southern California from sleepy Spokane in search of sun, opportunity, and drastically altered POV. A rental bungalow found in the then-derelict Ocean Park district of Santa Monica bode well despite insistent marine haze, portly rats tunneling in ivy-laden date palms, and dilapidated piers. We heard from neighbors right away which well-known beach cottage housed quarrelling Jane Fonda and Tom Hayden; of cheap studios rented by musicians, poets, writers, and rising artists like young Richard Diebenkorn painting what he saw from his soaring hillside perch above the ramshackle scene below. He'd just painted "Ocean Park #68" in shades of green, teal, blue, red-brown and peach when we arrived in 1974, yet we wouldn't see any of this series until much later, an L.A.-hour's drive away from where they'd emerged.

Next door on the weed-choked corner, just two short blocks from the sea, there lived an old crone who screeched at me over the backyard fence concerning her perceived agents of death, disease, and destruction—in particular naming the causes of cancer: for starters, birds visiting the garbage-pocked backyard she called an organic garden were more often shot than shooed, accused of harboring cancer "seeds". She'd begin shouting and aim her BB gun at me, claiming our rental was a "cancer house", the owner preceding us having succumbed to the ravages of metastasized breast cancer, the destiny of all women within its walls thereafter, she direly warned. Duly scared by that prospect, I took to roaming the rooms tuning into how someone might have suffered in them, superstitiously thinking how the neighbor may have contributed to the scenario: method to madness perhaps, her own fear fueling airborne "seeds" to doom inhabitants of the house. Once I came home from work and sensed an intruder had entered, taking nothing but moving the shadows about, searching for who knows what. The old woman said a ghost surely haunted the place, tortured soul of cancer's take, reminding future occupants these premises belonged truly to her whose life cut short still owned the sunsets through the stained-glass windows facing seaward.

Some nights the whirr of distant traffic merging with turning tides lulled us into innocent torpor, only to be wakened by flooding searchlights, the swoop and slap of L.A.P.D. helicopters nigh. Sometimes these were film crews shooting stock footage for television news, sometimes real cops chasing down a fugitive. Then in spring of that first year a shocking urban drama unraveled in nearby Compton the "martyrdom by fire" of six SLA members and maybe their hostage, Patty Hearst, inflamed by cops and FBI. As with infamous L.A. car-chases, local TV coverage fed viewers ongoing access to live details, hooking us on proximate peril.

On an especially gray and murky day our two guinea pig rescues grazing sweetly beneath a protective cage were savagely attacked by a pair of huge white mastiffs no one had seen before or ever would again. I'd gone out to check on them and found their cold little bodies, their cleanly broken necks, the ghostly dogs still peering at the mess, my wailing incomprehension piercing the leaden sky. Frightened, still I stood my ground, they jumped the fence into mist, and I thought to myself: What kind of life is this?

Did Diebenkorn looking down upon the world below his hillside studio witness these unfoldings beneath his brushes in serene shimmering strata of *pentimenti,* remarking on his stay in Ocean Park while listening to Bach? Seeing those paintings decades later on museum walls, I caught the refractions, the aura of ambiguity captured in calm intersections of lavenders and tender blues, shot through with light-filled tangerine dreams. Layered beneath I discerned rumors of the nation's young boys and men engaged in faraway wars, with maybe hints of more local skirmishes enlisting madwomen, ghosts, and politicians clattering noisily in the boundless boulevards of palm fronds.

Letter to God (After Hafiz)

How like you to speak to me of trees,
piercing the feathered air as if
poetry could teach the heart of loss,
convey the constancy of change.

So much flux breeds excess caution--
I'm still not at home with it-- how could
I be, who only wanted to love you,
as if it came to me naturally.

The mind that ever fears the worst
speaks volumes about its motives,
always asking what if and why not,
mainly intending, "Then show me!"

And that you do, more often than not
stranding me here on rock in sight
of sky: What now, Love, is this all?
Will you love me eternally?

If Emily Had Been So Stricken

My left chest has not a breast,
    but that's okay, I must confess,
because it tried to kill me.

My left arm is twice the size
    of my un-irradiated right,
yet another asymmetry.

At neuropathy that numbs my toes,
    fingers and calves, I thumb my nose
and curse the poison yew tree.

Revisions may well resume anon,
    for cancer's a mischievous con,
and I've an ill-starred chemistry.

Setting deviations apart,
    I'm counting with a beating heart
my days against eternity.

Malady as Metaphor

A Thank You Card

So this is how it is to be cancer's bitch,
edited parts of my former self left
on the cutting-room floor, teasing
significance from even the dullest
moments, trading hope for uncertainty,
most unusual promise you'll never leave
me—thanks for that last, although
we know I could've lived without it.

Mediation Meditation

Some wounds stay locked in a sort of cellular prison
confounding with apparent acts of resistance while
blocking further damage with stubborn-walled fear
so nothing can take place save the inevitable outcome
they call disease disguised as a dark intervention

Autograph Tree Rescue

Strange little woody pod,
sized and gnarled like my fist
caught me by surprise,
carelessly perched askew
beside grove of wind-cracked
screw-pines and patches of
pinkish sand, passively
poised to ride next high tide,
asleep for countless weeks.
I scooped you up, peered
at fleshy petals dried half-
opened to central whorl,
a twisty curving yellow
vortex stained reddish with
tender seeds, their residue
suggesting cyclic turn.

I couldn't put you down,
pocketed your artful form,
delivered you by plane instead.
Beached on opposite shore
across the wide Pacific sea,
you closed your stiffening
petals as if to cover
your nakedness. Attempting
to force them open I
heard a tiny warning creak
and decided then
to let you be. In time,
leaning sideways against
a sunny window facing

the ocean view some
silent stirring must have
compelled a prelude
to rebirthing. Nothing
came of it. Progeny
sustained by salty air
and sea did not survive
displacement, your arms
remaining ever open.

But quiet wisdom now
oddly fills the space:
I who selfishly
stole your rightful lives
and fruitful deaths, solely
to possess the beauty
of your sensual form,
to make you a metaphor,
cradled your leathery
remains, the rattling seeds
within, and knew your pain
as if it were my own.

How We Know

Wild animals have sometimes messaged
me—a fox, two hawks, a bear,
and five boars—not bad for a city dweller
mostly unable to break away.
I'm not really sure what they tried to tell me,
but I paid close attention and can't
forget how though unspoken I somehow
knew it was likely about my
beleaguered existence on earth—
my lifelong fear of having to leave it.

In their shining eyes I caught glimpses
of transitions I'd rather not see—
throes of father, mother, sister, and friends
who'd only wanted to make a good life,
expiring against deadline to make a good
death. First, surprise, then a brave fight,
gives way to confused resignation when
Reaper takes their breath away,
and dormant neurons awake to guide
their blinding passage to cosmic realms.

After all, what matters is of course not matter,
as surely those animal messengers
know. This planet's a place we landed for better
or worse, in sickness and in health,
yet it's not what we're wedded to. Captives and care-
takers, destined for recycling, our lives
intersect with creatures and landscapes
whose wildness was once our familial
own. We exchange carbon gifts among ourselves,
naming it love, not loss, in the end.

Stones of Tohono O'odham

Sunset on the Tohono O'odham rez
spreads wide swathes of coral
and turquoise above while Wendell walks
us around fields outside the modest
house. As the sky's light intensifies,
I catch glints of mineral pink and quartz
refractions off a ring of smooth squash-size
oval stones bordering the yard, ask
about them, stunned by their strange,
presence there, a faint illumined glow
charged by end of day light-change.

They're our ancestors' cooking stones,
he says, *ancient, found in the land
when fields were plowed, honored by us
today.* He bends to pick one up
and places it firmly in my hands, offers
it as a gift to take to our people
in San Juan Bautista, and beckons us
to share dinner with his family. Inside
his wife cooks beans and fry bread on iron
woodstove, fragrant, plentiful. Two
teenage boys and two young girls sit quietly
on a bunkbed in the open kitchen space.
We give thanks and eat as darkness
gathers over the deepening stones.

Back home the stone looks different,
its age and purpose more pronounced:
petrified grease and chipped, heavy
for its size. When I hold it, jolts of hidden

energy jar my idea of it toward
the visceral.

In oral tradition, Tohono O'odham tell
of Man in the Maze as stand-in for life,
a sacred puzzle to parse, wending
through blockages and passages —
choices — to his center. From there
he can see all that *was*, before
he's welcomed by the Sun God into
Next World. And a tempered
stone rests in a field of possibilities,
as primal sun cycles fire across
the desert dome.

Star Maps I

The warrior and the dreamer went out to sea
                in a rugged grey metal boat,
out with the tide from rainy Hilo, toward steep
                bright slopes of Kilauea
streaming her fiery ropes, billowing sulfur,
                smoke & molten lava,
into the glassine waters they rode on—
                so close they were, hot
flaming bubbles dinged the boat's bottom as
                sharp pops like bullets,
until their feet began to burn, throats raked,
                & lungs choking they beat
a swift retreat, though mesmerized, booming
                back to shore with ebb-tide,
waves reflecting giant gelatinous stars
                gleaming wildly like
brilliant upheaval of volcanic star-flow
                from troubled earth.
Warrior and dreamer knew how to read these star
                maps, landing homeward
on a sodden beach, alive to every current,
                returned to winter light.

Das Boot: Sixth Extinction Log

Note a lone fishing vessel
rocking in the ocean swells
like a seesaw, off the coast
of Maine. Ma Atlantic
delivers as best she can
scant scallop harvests
to this doughty trawler,
but it's pretty much bait
and switch, now that she's
almost all fished out.
Which is why the fishermen
had switched from cod
to scallops trapped in nets,
soon to vanish like all the rest.

They'll let bygones be bygones
anon, depart Ma's watery
grave to scour the sun-parched land;
become seekers of terrestrial
wash-ups until the face
of the earth is covered over
with living water again.

Crows Before the Fall

Do you remember the opulence
of peach and violet sunset,
how as we walked toward evening
a sudden muffled movement
disturbed our mutual trance?

First, ungainly flap of wings, then
soundless alighting of a dozen birds,
composed in stark contrast against
dusky cemetery landscape: black
crows becalmed on white crypts.
They didn't caw or fidget, only craned
their cunning heads. Jet marble
eyes reflect some hidden light, rapt,
poised to align with imminent arrival.

This moment like an old star
witnessing its destiny — radiance
subsumed into blackest black,
with cast of light and shadow:
before, after, again and again
and Now.

Request

Please
when I'm unable to
speak too sick to care
or in a coma or dead
remember I said
who I became is not
the result or composite
of all you who
remain will say I am
or was or will be
recalled as having been,
resignation
having shaped
a whole new list
of triumphs & sorrows
beyond telling,
no longer evident
in the morass you see
that in passing must
surrender freely
the idea of me at last
to we.

About The Author

Sometimes it takes a good fright to shake us out of our customary zone. Faced with serious illness, the lifelong poet who'd worked as educator, print journalist, network television story editor, museum curator, writer, and community arts advocate returned to her roots. The poems gathered in this chapbook were written over a recent six-year period during which she consulted with the "home" elements of earth, wind, fire, and water, calling on them to guide her poetic rendering of what genuinely matters, no matter what. What emerges from what she calls the willing dirt is a living testimony on behalf of a life lived passionately in love with the natural world while attempting to make peace with a material world much in need of it.

Her poems, essays, print articles and columns, book and film reviews have been published in many literary journals, daily and weekly newspapers, magazines and periodicals over several decades. She lives in California's South Bay Area. Visit her at www.jadebradbury.com

www.ingramcontent.com/pod-product-compliance
Lightning Source LLC
Chambersburg PA
CBHW060344080526
44584CB00013B/914